To dear f[...]

On the occasion of
your first holy communion
With love from Min

children's Letters to GOD

children's Letters to GOD

The New Collection

Compiled by Stuart Hample and Eric Marshall
Illustrated by Tom Bloom

Kyle Cathie Limited

Book design by Tom Starace
Illustrations by Tom Bloom
Cover design by Rebecca Foster

A CIP Catalogue record for this book is available from the British Library

First published in Great Britain in 1992 by
Kyle Cathie Limited
122 Arlington Road, London NW1 7HP
general.enquiries@kyle-cathie.com
www.kylecathie.com

This edition published in 2006

Published in the United States by
Workman Publishing, New York

ISBN 978 1 85626 682 6

Printed in Singapore

10 9 8 7 6 5

Contents

The letters in this book express that part of a child's world reserved for special thoughts and wishes. The subject matter ranges through those beliefs, desires, questions and doubts that are urgent and common to all children. Some of the letters are disarmingly wise, others naive; some are knowing, some simple; some reverent, some not so reverent. Many are weighted with seriousness; others are lit with smiles. All of them are addressed to God with much hope and trust.

Grownups know for certain, of course, that the letters will not get there no matter how much postage they carry. But then grownups know so much more than children—sometimes.

In choosing these letters, we've tried to convey the incredible variety they represent. Their spelling and grammar have not been corrected, for what they say they say better as they are.

—Eric Marshall and Stuart Hample

Puzzlements, dilemmas and other imponderables

In Sunday School they told us what you do. Who does it when you are on holiday?

Jane

How did you know you were God?

Charlene

Dear God,

I read the bible. What does begat mean? Nobody will tell me.

Love,
Alison

Dear God,
On Holloween I am
going to wear a Devil's
costume, Is that
all night with you?

Marnie

Dear God.
Are you really invisible or is that just a trick

Lucy

Dear God,

Is it true my father Won't get in Heaven if he uses his Bowling Words in the house?

Anita

Dear God,

Did you mean for giraffe to look like that or was it an accident.

Norma

Dear God,
Instead of Letting people die
and haveing to Make new ones
why don't you just
keep the ones you got now?

Jane

Dear God,
   Who draws the lines
   around the countries?

   Nan

Dear God,

Do animals use you or is there somebody else for them?

Nancy

Dear God,

I went to this wedding and they kissed right in church. Is that ok?

Neil

Dear God
Are there any
Patriarchs around
today?
Patrick

Dear God
I like the Lords prayer best of all.
Did you have to write it a lot or
did you get it right the first time?
I have to write everything I ever
write over again.

Lois

God,
IT'S O.K. That you
made different
religions but
don't you get
mixed up some-times.

Arnold

Dear God
In bible times
did they really
talk that fancy?

Jennifer

Dear God,

I would like to know why all the things you said are in red?

Joanne

Dear God

What does it mean you are a jealous God. I thought you had everything

Jane

Dear God,

Is reverend Coe a friend of yours, or do you just know him through business?

Donny

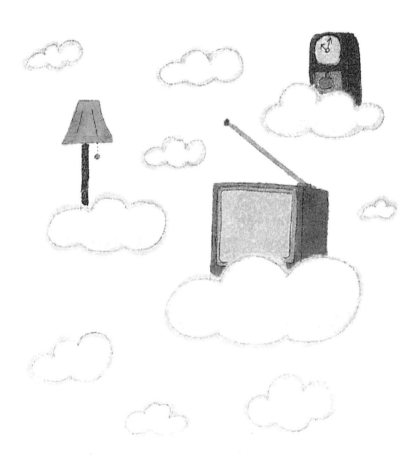

Dear God,
Do you know about things
before their invented?

Charles

Did You Really Mean Do UNto
Others As They Do UNTO You,
Because If You Did Then I'm
Going to Fix My Brother.

Darla

Dear God,
   When you made the first
man did he work as
good as we do now?
                        Tom

Dear God
My Grandpa says you were around when he was a little boy. How far back do you go?

Love
Dennis

Dear God,

I know all about where babies come from. I think. From inside mommies and daddies put them there.

Where are they before that? Do you have them in heaven? How do they get down here? Do you have to take care of them all first. Please answer all my questions. I always think of you.

Yours truly
Susan

Dear God,
I am English
what are you?
Robert

Fervent wishes, suggestions and complaints

Dear God,
Thank you for
the baby brother
but what I prayed
for was a Puppy

Joyce

DeaR God
How Come you didn't
invent any new animals
lately? We still have
Just all the old ones.

Johny

Dear God—
Please put another Holiday between Christmas and Easter. There is nothing good in there now.

Ginny

Dear God,
   It rained for are whole
holiday and is my father
mad! He said some things
about you that people are
not supposed To say, but I
hope you will not hurt him
anyway.
                    Your friend
        But I am not going To Tell you
                who I am

Dear God
Why is Sunday
School on Sunday?
I thought it
was suppose to
be our day of rest.
Tom L.

Please Send me Pony I never ask for anything before you Can Look it up

Bruce

Dear Mr. God

I wish you would not make it so easy for people to come apart. I had 3 stitches and a shot.

Janet

Dear God,

How come you did all those miracles in the old days and don't do any now?

Seymour

Dear -God- if-
we-come-back
as -something-
please-don't
le t-me-be
Jennifer-Horton
because-I-hate
her.

Denise

Dear God,
If you give me
genie lamp like Alladin
I will give you anything
you want
except my money
or my chess set.
Raphael

Dear God,

My brother is a rat. You should give him a tail. Ha. ha.

Danny

Dear God,
Please Send Dennis Clark

to a different camp
this year.

Peter

Dear God,
I wish that there wasn't
no such thing of sin.

I wish that there was
not no such thing
of war.

Tim M
age 9

Dear God

Maybe Cain and Abel
would not kill each so much
if they had their own rooms.
It works with my brother

Larry

Dear God,
   I want to be just like my Daddy when I get big but not with so much hair all over.

                    Sam

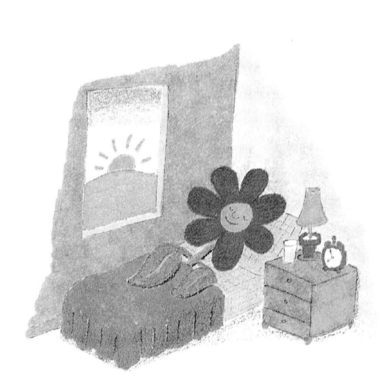

Dear God,
  I keep waiting for Spring but
it never come yet. Don't
forget.

     Mark

Approvals, confidences and thanks

You don't have to worry about me. I always look both ways

Dean

Dear God,
I think the stapler
is one of your
greatest invention

Ruth M.

Dear God,
My name is Simon. Thats from the bible. I am eight and a half. We live across the street from the park. I have a dog name buster. I used to have a hamster but he got out and ran away. I am small for my age My hobbies are swimming, bowling, my chemistry set reading, coin collecting and tropical fish. Right now I have three kinds. Well I guess I said a Mouthful, Goodbye.

Always a friend

Simon

Dear God,
I think about you sometimes even when I'm not praying

Elliott

Dear God,
I bet it is
very hard.
for you to
love all of
every body in the
whole world
There are only
4 people in our
family and I
can never do it.

Nan

Dear God

Of all the people who work for you I like Peter and John the best.

Rob

Dear God,
My brother told me
about being born
but it doesn't
sound right.
Marsha

Dear God,

If you watch in Church on Sunday I will show you my new Shoes

Mickey D.

Dear God,

I like the story about Chanuka the best of all of them.
You really made up some good ones.

Glenn

GOD,
I WOULD LIKE
TO O LIVE
900 YEARS LIKE THE
GUY IN THE BIBLE
LOVE,
CHRIS

Dear God
I love You.
how are You fine.
Im fine to
My Mother has five girls
And one Boy,
I am one of them.
Nancy 6

Dear God

I don't ever feel alone since I found out about you.

Nora

We read Thos. Edison
made light.
But in Sun. School They said
You did it.
So I bet he stoled
your Idea.
Sincerly,
Donna

Dear God,

If you let The dinasor not exstinct we would not have a country.

You did the right thing.

Jonathan

Dear God. here's a poem

I Love You
Because you give
us what we need to live
But I wish you
would tell me why
you made it so
we have to die.

Daniel (age 8)

Dear God
It is great
the way
you always
get the
Stars in
the right
places.

Jeff

God: the bad people
laghed at noah— you
make an ark on dry
land you fool. But
he was smart he stuck
with you. thats what
I would do.

Eddie

Dear God,
I do not think anybody
could be a better
God. Well I just
want you to know but
I am not just saying
that because you
are God. Charles

Dear God,

I didn't think orange went with purple until I saw the sunset you made on Tue. That was <u>Cool</u>.

EUGENE

Dear God,
I am doing
the best I can.

Frank